W9-BMU-322

PREPARING FOR PEER PRESSURE

A Guide for Parents of Young Children

James B. Stenson

Scepter Publishers
Princeton, NJ 08542

Nihil obstat:
    Daniel V. Flynn, JCD
    Censor librorum
Imprimatur:
    Patrick J. Sheridan
    Vicar-General
    Archdiocese of New York

August 1, 1988

Books by James B. Stenson:

— *Upbringing: A Discussion Handbook for Parents of Young Children*

— *Lifeline: The Religious Upbringing of Your Children*

— *Preparing for Adolescence: Answers for Parents*

— *Preparing for Peer Pressure: A Guide for Parents of Young Children*

— *Successful Fathers*

Available from Scepter Publishers
(800) 322-8773 or www.scepterpublishers.org

Preparing for Peer Pressure was originally published as Scepter Booklet No. 177.

© 1988 Scepter Publishers

This edition © 2001 Scepter Publishers

Printed in the United States of America

ISBN 1-889334-36-7

Contents

L ET ME SAY at the outset what this book is
not. This is not a "how-to" set of guidelines for parents of high-school age children. It
does not deal with issues of "adolescent man-
agement" — curfews, allowances, rules for
dating, coping with inroads of the pop/drug culture, and the like. All of these are part of an
overriding and at times urgent question to
countless families: How can parents effectively
guide and discipline young people who have
most of the powers of adulthood but almost no
maturity of judgment or serious sense of responsibility?

Parents of grown children need a broader
treatment of this subject than we can give in

these few pages. What they need is a book, or several books. Or, from a practical standpoint, perhaps what they most need is to befriend older couples who can give them concrete advice based on their own recent experience with teen-agers. These would be people who have done a manifestly good job in raising their own children — that is, parents whose children have grown to become competent, responsible men and women who live by Christian principles.

If you ask such people (as I have) how they managed to cope with peer-pressure influences on their children's values, you would notice a recurring factor: They started young. When their children were still infants or grade-schoolers, they established a clear framework of guidance and discipline, thus consciously forming their children's conscience and char-acter. This firm and intelligent leadership held sway in their children's lives all the way through adolescence. There were problems, to be sure, but the children emerged into adulthood with their values intact. As grown men and women, they now honor their parents (as God com-mands all of us to do) by living according to their principles.

This book is intended for younger parents, people whose children are under 12. It is never too soon for such couples to be concerned about their children's future life as responsible adults. Happiness in life will depend, in very large measure, on how well the children handle themselves in an environment of irreligion, sexual permissiveness, and unrestrained pursuit of pleasure. Coping with the forces of materialism has to begin long before the onset of puberty — as countless parents have found to their dismay. Neglect in the younger years can have serious, and even tragic, consequences.

What young couples need is a long-term strategy for their children's upbringing. This book is an attempt to help form such a strategy, or at least to make a forceful start in that direction. Strategy usually begins with asking a few clear questions: Where are we now? Where do we want to go? How can we best get from here to there?

These pages will not provide easy answers to these questions. There are none. What we hope to do is provide some thought-provoking material for discussion. It's been said that, if questions are posed in a reflective and concrete way, the solutions generally suggest themselves. In our experience, parents badly need to do much more of this kind of thinking together. What sort of young men and women do they want their children to become, and what needs to be done now to make that ideal — with God's help — a reality?

I've used the word "experience" here. Let me explain.

I have worked for 20 years as a school administrator and teacher. In that capacity, I have known hundreds of families, in many cases quite intimately. I have talked extensively to parents, young people, priests, teachers, coaches, and personal counselors. My colleagues and I have seen hundreds of young people grow from infancy to adulthood. We have seen many turn out very well; others we have seen meet with serious trouble in life, even tragedy. In quite a few families, we could see young children headed for serious trouble later. All the danger-signals pointed toward adolescent crisis.

In short, we have seen many parents make a lot of serious mistakes, mostly through neglect and thoughtlessness. It is this experience with others' mistakes that forms the material in these pages. The ideas and observations spelled out here have come from the conscientious concern of many knowledgeable people. You, as parents, can profit from what we've learned.

If the observations here seem somewhat negative in slant, there are two good reasons for this. First, the problem is urgently serious and our discussion here is really a kind of warning. Secondly, negative guidelines lead to greater freedom of action. Nobody can articulate a clear and positive recipe for raising children right; no two families are exactly alike. But it's very useful to know what to avoid. Any long-term mapping of a journey (in this case a strategy for a course of action) requires knowledge of pitfalls, obstacles, and dead-ends. These, unfortunately, are all too common in family life today. Learning to avoid the mistakes of others, or at least wanting to do so, is already a major contribution to your children's future happiness.

The Biggest Problem:
Thinking Ahead

If you were to consult adults who deal professionally with the problems of young people — teachers, college and high-school counselors, clergymen, marriage counselors, drug-rehabilitation specialists — you would probably find a common consensus about the fundamental problem underlying young people's troubled lives. They would tell you that the parents of these young people were uninformed, not to say naive, about the scope and magnitude of the forces pitted against their children's values during adolescence. Consequently, though the parents fed and clothed and cared for their children, they had done little or nothing to strengthen their children's character. Lacking this thing called strength of character, the children were pushovers for the forces outside the family.

Of course, it's rather easy to see why parents today can lack this foresight. A home with small children is a very busy place, and there is scarcely time to think seriously about anything long-term. Shopping, budgeting, homework, housework, leisure pursuits, driving the kids all over the map and back, sticking to a tight schedule — these activities can easily crowd out thought. And the kids are so happily busy, so charming in their carefree play, that it's hard to imagine them as grown-up adults, 15 or 20 years later, meeting with serious personal problems — even, as is increasingly likely, with divorce. In our experience, parents almost never consider how highly probable it is that their children could someday be divorced. Their children, not somebody else's.

The statistics are sobering. Let's take the numbers for a moment and put them into more concrete terms. Imagine, if you will, a schoolyard filled with about 500 young children, happily at play — among them your own. They run and laugh, they play ball and skip rope. If current statistics hold true over the next 20 years (and there's no reason to predict otherwise), the following will happen to this group of children:

- 60% will stop practicing their religion altogether; they will have no faith to pass on to their children — your grandchildren.

- 100% will be extensively exposed to socially accepted pornography, with all that this implies about respect for the opposite sex and the sanctity of marriage.

- 60–70% will experience premarital sexual relations.

- 20–40% will live cohabitationally before marriage.

- 100% will be actively solicited to try drugs sometime in high school or college.

- 10%, at least, will have serious addictive problems with alcohol or other drugs.

- 10–20% will experience serious psychological problems, notably clinical depression.

- of those with drug or psychological problems, a small number will take their lives — a small statistic but a devastating tragedy to loved ones left behind.

- 50%, fully one-half of the 500 children, will be divorced by the age of 30.

Ask any professional who works with these problems and he will tell you: Every damaged young person, every spiritually troubled young adult in his or her 20's, was once a carefree and busy child playing happily in a schoolyard. But the root problems were at work even then.

What parents don't seem to realize is that

problems later in life — with faith, morality, marital stability — do not come about overnight. And, emphatically, they do not come about merely through subversive peer influences. What is done, or not done, in childhood directly influences how well or poorly the children will resist the pressures of materialism, the temptation to abandon traditional Christian values and conform to a different vision of life.

What is this materialism? Simply put, it is the belief that man is merely a thing. The purpose of life, therefore, is the pursuit of pleasure and the avoidance of pain. Spiritual values, including the rights of God and the inherent dignity of other people, are illusory, man-made structures, mere social conventions. Other people, therefore, may be treated like things. There's no life after death, and therefore no final accountability for the way we've lived.

These notions are seldom so badly articulated, but they are found implicitly all around us. They are a widespread and growing influence on family life in Western societies. They are the environment that surrounds today's children.

Children entering adolescence acquire virtually boundless new opportunities for pleasure, power, and escape into illusion. So strong is the natural urge to conform, and so powerfully seductive are the temptations toward indulgence, that children simply must have a powerful inner strength of will to resist. Peer pressures are only permanently successful when they move into a vacuum in the children's inner character.

The peer-pressure problem, therefore, is not one of merely avoiding "bad companions." That's virtually impossible these days. The key question really is: Why is a child attracted irresistibly to such companions in the first place?

Some adolescents give in to the pressures. Others resist or ignore them. What is the key difference between these two groups? In our experience, it is simply strength of character.

A well-formed conscience, a firm religious belief, a prayerful relationship with God, a trust in his parents' powers of judgment, a lifetime habit of self-control (saying "no" to one's feelings), a respect for the rights of others — all these traits firm up a young person's will to resist. They lead ultimately to real happiness and success in life.

But, to put it bluntly, countless children are growing up without them. In our experience, parents who do not work consciously to teach their children these things — by word and by their own example — are asking for big trouble.

Character Formation:
A Brief Sketch

We've used the terms "character" and "formation" here. Let's clarify them a bit.

Let's step away for a moment from the warm sentiments that young children evoke in all of us. It is easy to be moved by children's charming simplicity. Their fresh young lives are immensely attractive, even enviable, and it's tempting to wish that they would always stay so happy. The powerful parental instincts to protect and nuture make it hard for us to withstand a youngster's tears, sorrow, and disappointment.

But to look at the children's future realistically, we have to be more objective. We have to see the children's nature as it really is, and to look coldly at what can happen to it.

Realistically speaking, young children are essentially self-centered, self-preoccupied little creatures who are given over to gratifying their appetites and passions, and who seek, wherever possible, to impose their will on others around them. They are naturally takers, not givers. Of course, they are cute and charming about this manipulation, but the self-centered drives are always there.

"Formation" is everything that parents do and say to avoid having their children grow up this way. The children must be taught to say "thank you," then later to mean "thank you," and then later to give of their goods generously. They are formed patiently, by teaching and practice, from being takers to givers. Formation is, in other words, an education in values and in strengths of character.

This process does not occur spontaneously. It has to be made to happen. The collective experience of mankind in this matter is pretty straightforward: If children are not formed in strengths of character — by parents, schools, and society — they will grow up to be larger versions of what they were as youngsters. They will remain egocentric, domineering, pleasure-seeking, and more-or-less irresponsible.

To look at it another way, character is the sum total of what Christian civilization has called the virtues: faith, hope, charity, prudence, justice, fortitude, and temperance. All other virtues (piety, industriousness, honesty, loyalty, etc.) derive from these.

We don't use all these terms today, but we have a common-sense understanding of the concepts. These seven strengths of character form a useful framework for evaluating children's character or lack thereof. To be more specific:

Faith — belief in God and in all that he has taught through his Church.

Hope — confidence that God will give us the means to eternal salvation. (For Christians, hope's symbol has been the anchor, the tie that holds us fast through the storms of life.)

Charity — love for God and for all people, with the love of God being the number one principle in life and thus determining all other loves and attractions.

Prudence — sound judgment, an ability to make the important distinctions in life: good from evil, truth from falsehood, the important from the trivial, the eternal from the transitory. (A well-formed conscience belongs here.)

Justice — a sense of responsibility; giving others their due, starting with God.

Fortitude — personal toughness; an ability to endure or overcome pain, discomfort, inconvenience, disappointment.

Temperance — self-control; an ability to overcome "feelings" for the sake of a higher good; an ability to use pleasurable things moderately and reasonably; rational control of the appetites.

We all know character when we see it in people. It is what makes us respect them and admire them. Contrary to what many parents think, these strengths of character do not develop unaided and of themselves in the lives of their children. The acquisition of character takes years of conscious teaching and exercised practice. Without this preparation for life, children at the age of 14 can't be expected to defend themselves effectively against assaults on their faith, their chastity, their intentions to live rightly and honorably. They simply do not have the strength.

Home Life

Plenty of young people can and do exercise these strengths of character. My colleagues and I have known great numbers of adolescents and young adults who are responsible, considerate, self-disciplined, confident, and deeply religious. They are the kind of young men and women whom parents would like to have, sometime in the future, as spouses for their grown children. (Though parents don't always have a clear picture of what their own children should be as adults, they usually have high standards for their future sons-in-law and daughters-in-law. It's not a bad way of evaluating young people — starting, of course, with one's own children.)

In our experience, young adults like this have come almost invariably from homes where the parents (sometimes only a single parent) have certain personal characteristics. The parents have deep religious convictions; they take their faith seriously. They are actively concerned about the formation of their children's conscience and character. They practice self-sacrifice themselves, and their children know it. They are savvy about the culture their children are growing up in. Their children see them as strong and confident people, and therefore admirable, worthy of being imitated. They do not live as mere "consumers."

My colleagues and I have seen it both ways. We have also seen youngsters overcome by the allurements of materialism, as described above. We have seen young people lose their faith, lack a purpose in life, or get into serious marital difficulties. We have seen tragic alcohol-related accidents, serious dependence on drugs, and even some suicides.

It's not fair to say, of course, that in every case the home life was responsible for these problems. The forces of materialism are so powerful, and young people so frequently defenseless, that casualties can happen anywhere. In the 1960's and '70s especially, the climate of irreligion and institutionalized hedonism arose so swiftly that many parents were taken entirely by surprise. The children were lost to these forces before the parents grew aware of what was happening.

Nevertheless, today we can safely say that adolescents with peer-pressure problems (that is, children with weaker characters) generally have been raised in homes with certain traits in common. My associates and I have noticed enough similarities in the family environments of these troubled youngsters so that we can make some qualified generalizations here. In our experience, trouble in the adolescent years can usually be predicted (not absolutely always, but very frequently) when the children are younger. What are some of these "danger signals" in the children's home environment?

- Parents give in easily and habitually to children's wishes and "feelings," even when they judge that this might be a mistake. They frequently permit what they do not approve of. Children thus learn to let their desires override judgments of conscience; "feelings" and impulses become a guide for action.

- Children have a low tolerance for inconvenience or discomfort; they have a horror of physical pain. They can successfully plead and badger their way out of uncomfortable commitments: music lessons, Scouting, appointments, deadlines. (Historical fact: As a child, Beethoven despised his piano studies. His parents forced him to persevere.)

- Children have too much spending money. They habitually overindulge in soft drinks, sweets, fast food, and junk food. They can pretty much consume what they want whenever they want, and they do.

- Parents are minimal in the practice of religious sacrifice. Though the family may attend church regularly, this is done mostly as routine custom. There is little or no prayer in family life, no evident love for God. Children do not see parents living a sense of responsibility toward a clear-cut internalized ethic. In the children's eyes, parents do not seem responsible to anything, except perhaps a relentlessly busy calendar.

- Members of the family get dressed up for parties and for guests, but not for church.

- The father, especially, is not a strong moral figure in the home. He defers "children's things" to his wife. The children see him engaged almost exclusively in leisure activities and minor home repairs. He does not show much overt respect and gratitude toward his wife. (Experience indicates, by the way, that children's attitudes toward each parent mirror the parents' attitudes toward each other. Children show little respect for parents who show little respect for one another.)

- Children know almost nothing about their parents' personal histories, and nothing at all about grandparents. They have almost no idea how their parents earn a living.

- Dinner-table conversation is almost exclusively about pleasures (food, entertainment, TV, etc.) or is negative criticism and gossip about people. There is no prayer before meals.

- Children show little or no respect for people outside the family: guests, friends of parents, teachers, salespeople, the elderly. They have to be persistently reminded to show good manners in public: "please" and "thank you" are not habitually part of their speech. At Christmas, the children rip through a small mountain of presents, but they do not write or say "thank you" to relatives.

- Children complain persistently about situations that can't be helped: weather, reasonable delays, physical discomfort, personality differences, etc. Their most common word of complaint is "boring."

Since their lives are managed, rather than directed, they are accustomed to having problems solved by oversolicitous adults. They thus learn to escape problems, not solve them; they learn to shun discomfort, not endure it. (A habit of escape like this is dangerous in later life; alcohol and drugs and divorce are efficient escape devices.)

- Ironically, for all the parents' efforts to provide a comfortable home, the children have little respect for them. The kids see their parents as "nice," and they will admit that they "like" Mom and Dad most of the time. They simply do not see their parents as strong, and therefore admirable, people. When asked whom they do admire, they will give a long list of entertainment and sports figures. (Children with strong characters, on the other hand, invariably have high respect for their parents.)

- Children have no serious hobbies except television-watching or listening to music. Their thinking is dominated by television culture. They know the words to dozens of commercials, but they don't know the Ten Commandments.

- Parents watch television indiscriminately. They allow "adult entertainment," especially through cable TV, into the home. Though they may restrict, more or less, the children's access to this soft porn, they are driving home a powerful and dangerous ethical message to the children: "When you're old enough, anything goes." Sex-as-recreation, therefore, is not treated as something objectively wrong for everyone; it is simply inappropriate for children. The good-evil dichotomy becomes a question of age.

- Children (older ones especially) form opinions almost entirely on the basis of vague impressions. They are easily swayed by emotional appeals and superficial appearances. They do not recognize claptrap — commercial, political, ideological — when they see it.

- Children never ask the question "Why?" except to defy directions from legitimate authority. They are intellectually dull, showing little serious curiosity about life outside the family-school universe. In school, they are often incorrigibly poor spellers; that is, they are habitually careless in work and do not take correction seriously.

- Children have little or no concern about causing embarrassment to the family. There is no cultivated sense of "family honor." If public dress and deportment cause shame to the parents, that's just too bad.

- The worst punishment the children will receive at home is a long, boring lecture or a moderately troublesome "grounding." Punishment, moreover, is inconsistent in severity and application.

- Children have little sense of time. They scarcely ever have to wait for something, much less earn it. They have unrealistic expectations about the time necessary to complete something; they estimate either too much or too little. Large tasks are thus put off too long, or small jobs appear monstrous. There is almost no concept of deadline, or of working steadily within a self-initiated time frame. This is important: Time-management is, after all, just another term for self-control. Children who are over-managed can grow out of touch with reality. Lacking a sense of how their powers can cope with problems, they lack confidence and they increasingly shun responsibilities. In the long run, this can have disastrous consequences, especially for the peace and stability of their marriage.

Please do not assume from this picture that children susceptible to peer pressure are all arrogant and bumptious brats, obvious targets for materialistic takeover. This is not the case.

Most often, the children from homes like this are just the opposite in appearance. They are typically cheery and well-scrubbed, pleasant and smiling, often very active (but only for the things they like). They are affectionate and sentimental and eager to please (up to a point); they are used to pleasant sentiments. They like to be liked, and indeed they expect it. They seem accustomed to dealing with adults as equals, and thus appear naively ignorant of respectful good manners. With a few troubled exceptions, they seem carefree; and indeed most of them are, entirely so.

Yet at the center of all these pleasant young people, more manifestly as they approach adolescence, there is something missing. Where there should be a firm conscience, there is a tangle of vague sentiments. Where there should be a purposeful will, there are shifting reactions to stimuli. Where there should be some desire to assume grown-up responsibilities, there is a hope — indeed an expectation — of prolonging childhood's pleasures indefinitely. Where there should be strength of character, there is a vulnerable little child, headed for trouble.

Patterns of Malformation

The outline drawn above (of what might be called a malformational home) is a composite sketch, not a comprehensive description. No two families are exactly alike, and trouble can derive from anywhere. Many tightly knit and pious families have had serious problems with their children. And, conversely, children from comfortable homes have often turned out quite well. As with any generalization about human life, there are exceptions.

Nevertheless, the features outlined above have reappeared so often in the history of so many troubled young adults that we are compelled to assume a cause-and-effect relationship.

What has gone wrong in these families? Why is it that so many children from pleasantly permissive and religiously lukewarm homes have caved in so easily to materialism? Is there a discernible pattern of mistakes made by the children's parents?

My associates and I think there is such a pattern. We think that many parents unwittingly make several serious and ongoing mistakes that result directly in their children's malformation. Let me explain these briefly here.

1. Parents simply do not think enough about what kind of men and women they want their children to become.

When they do think of their children's future, those thoughts center mainly (in fact, almost entirely) on college and career. They think of what their children will do, not what they will be.

Up until the early part of this century, parents did not concern themselves overmuch with their children's occupational futures. For centuries, parents knew what their children would do; they would do whatever their own parents did. Farmer's sons would become farmers; shoemakers' sons would be shoemakers; lawyers' sons would be apprenticed at law. Everybody's daughters would, of course, become homemakers. To be sure, there were exceptions. But by and large the children's course of occupation was reasonably set and not much considered.

Consequently, when parents up to our time thought of their children's futures, they thought in terms of character: Will my son be honored and respected for his integrity, his hard work, his responsibilities as breadwinner and citizen? Will he bring honor to us, his parents? Will our daughter be chaste and modest, giving us grandchildren to delight our old age? Will all our children marry well? Will some of them, please God, find a vocation to the service of the Church?

These questions, and others like them, determined the teaching and correction and self-discipline imposed at home. Since life involved so many risks, and since suffering clarified our human limitations, a firm trust in God was a critically important part of the family spirit. People prayed together.

As we have seen, and can see all around us, this sort of parental vision is no longer common. Parents think of their children's careers and the educational paths leading thereto. They think little about their children's self-control, will power, self-confidence, religious convictions, or commitment to chastity. They think little about how these traits will affect the permanence and happiness of their children's future marriage.

The irony of this displaced concern (as any psychiatrist or marriage counselor can testify) is that young adults' serious personal problems are hardly ever directly job-related. There are plenty of young working people, successful and well-paid, whose personal lives are a wreck. People's personal unhappiness has seldom come from occupational complications. In fact, the exact reverse has usually been the case, where personal character flaws (drugs, psychological distress, marital troubles) have adversely affected job performance. Character, it seems, is more important than career.

It seems odd to us that parents think so little of their children's future marriage. As noted before, parents hardly ever foresee divorce as a clear and highly probable danger to their children's happiness, not to mention their own. It's a tragic fact: When your children divorce, you may suffer the permanent estrangement of your grandchildren. The courts don't much consider the visiting rights of grandparents.

Those parents who still retain the age-old concern for their children's future character (and there are many such parents) generally do a much better job raising their children. They have an idea, in fact a set of ideals, for their children's growth in character. They want their children to be strong — firm in faith, firm in judgment, firm in their sense of responsibility. Though this teaching process brings problems and hard work, it is worth it. Children can resist the pressures that would undo the family's values. By and large, with few exceptions, the children grow up to their expectations. They are responsible and honorable men and women who live by their parents' principles.

When God calls parents before his judgment, he will ask how well they have discharged their duties. He will ask how well the children have been taught to know him, to love him, and to serve him.

God will not ask what tax-bracket the kids are in, or what they got on their SAT's.

2. Parents don't seem to realize the long-term damage they can do by indulging their children's whims and appetites.

It's hard for many parents to grasp that "no" is also a loving word. And children simply must hear it from time to time. If the children do not experience loving denial, they cannot form the concept of self-denial. To arrive at adolescence these days without a well-formed internal power of self-denial is positively dangerous.

Adolescents can't "say No to drugs" if they're unfamiliar with the word. Bumper stickers are no substitute for a conscience.

Drugs and alcohol and sex are sources of powerfully pleasurable feelings. Even for strong-willed adolescents with firm habits of self-control, these temptations are tough to turn away from. For teens with a lifelong habit of parent-supported indulgence, these new and marvelous sensations are practically irresistible. Since infancy, these youngsters' lives have centered around their feelings. Why should they, how can they, say no to themselves now — now, of all times, when unprecedented possibilities for pleasure are opening up to their grasp?

Even aside from the danger of drug and alcohol involvements, the children's future marriages are put at risk.

Children who've known nothing but comfort, amusement, and self-preoccupation have a notoriously low tolerance for inconvenience and hardship. Ask any teacher. Children raised to be "happy" and "self-fulfilled," rather than strong and self-reliant, are out of practice in handling difficult or insoluble problems. Strong children learn either to solve such problems as best they can or to live with them, come what may. Weak children don't know what to do. They expect the problems to go away, as they always have somehow. And if the problems will not go away, then they will. They will somehow escape.

But marriage, especially in the first few years, inevitably brings difficult and even insoluble problems. One's spouse, like all other human beings, has faults that can sometimes pose difficulties. Young married people of strong character can live with these problems, letting their love override the differences and inconveniences inherent in any close human relationship. The weak, on the other hand, exaggerate the problems and eventually judge them to be intolerable. Escape is found through separation and eventually through the courts.

Priests and marriage counselors shake their heads at the increasingly trivial and petty problems that seem to be pulling recent marriages apart. Something is working destruction here. Perhaps it's the young people's expectation that life will continue as it always has been — comfortable and hassle-free. There is no such life, of course, but the kids don't seem to know this.

3. Parents rely too much on institutional and societal structures to do their job for them.

Even parents who are aware that some sort of character formation should be going on in their children's lives are misinformed about the help they can expect from outside the family. The support that was there until quite recently has greatly diminished or has almost disappeared entirely.

Less than a generation ago, parents could rely quite heavily on various institutions to teach their children right from wrong and to firm up the children's character through disciplined activity. Church schools and religious-instruction programs had a clear sense of mission and a comprehensive moral/doctrinal training. They may have overemphasized role-instruction, but at least they got the job done. Schools, generally speaking, made demands on the children's powers. Society, for all its faults, was fundamentally decent in its ethos: What was grossly immoral was also illegal.

For the last several decades in Western societies, parents could be excused for letting much of their children's upbringing be handled by these institutions. A neglect at home could be compensated for in school. Why bother to teach catechism extensively at home when the religion teachers can do the job professionally? Why take the kids to confession regularly when this will be done routinely at school? Why teach about premarital sex when the whole society frowns upon it? Why worry about life in college dormitories when the dorm supervisors will act in loco parentis, enforcing the same values as the home?

Having been raised in this same environment, or at least the tail-end of it in the 1960's, today's parents seem unaware of the sweeping societal and moral changes that have come about so quickly. More critically, they don't realize the implications these have on what their children are learning, or not learning, outside the family. The habits of trust and benign neglect in the last few generations simply do not apply any longer. What the children do not learn at home, they may not learn outside the home either. The end result is a doctrinal and moral and disciplinary vacuum.

The Church's structures of religious education are currently in serious disarray. This confusion has happened many times in the history of the Church, especially in periods of prolonged prosperity. Sooner or later it will pass, as it has before. In very many places, conscientious religious instructors are still valiantly teaching the traditional moral precepts of the Church. But elsewhere, much more broadly than people suspect, there is confusion and outright aberration. The current generation of children are caught in the middle.

The schools, too, by any objective standards, are simply not doing the job that they used to do. For various philosophical and political reasons, schools do not make the same serious and reasonably rigorous demands on children that were standard operating procedure for decades. In everything from penmanship to memorization to skills in calculating, children were made to form the concept of responsible performance to a set of standards. This is, unfortunately, no longer the case.

In fairness, it must be added here that conscientious teachers in today's schools meet with many frustrations of their own. They find it difficult, to say the least, to make demands on children whose home lives are suffocatingly comfortable. They often judge, quite rightly, that their efforts to impart "job-performance" responsibilities in the children are unsupported by the parents. Some intellectual accomplishments take hard work — period. Too many children have no concept of the term.

As for society at large, there have been drastic changes in the moral climate. Pornography is big business, permitted by the law and supported by the public. Our best-known corporations put their advertising dollars in sexually explicit commercials. And who would have guessed, 25 years ago, that abortion mills would one day be listed in the Yellow Pages.

The upshot of all these changes is simply this: If the children do not learn values and discipline at home, they are unlikely to learn these things anywhere. And where will that leave them?

4. Parents underestimate the power of example in their children's lives. They don't realize how little good example, and how much bad example, the children see.

Unlike previous ages in history, children today hardly ever see their parents work, especially their fathers. The home now centers around comfort and leisure activities. Since the real-life problems of the office and workplace are almost never brought home, the children have practically no notion of what adult-level responsibilities are like. The strengths that fathers exercise in the fulfillment of their jobs — dealing with deadlines, difficult problems, unreasonable bosses and customers are hardly ever witnessed by the children. If boys and girls only see Dad at rest, they have trouble forming a concept of manly responsibility in the outside world. Moreover, they may form the notion that enjoyment comes only from leisure and amusement, not from hard-won accomplishment, a job well done. The grown-up world of work thus becomes an unknown and vaguely threatening entity, looming in the distant future. This is not much incentive for wanting to grow up.

If the parents, enjoying a comfortable and apparently hassle-free life, do not display much personal strength to the children, then who does? Who are the heroes? Who are the people outside the family who embody strength of character, people whom society puts before the children to emulate?

For centuries our culture presented young people with models to imitate, figures who did great things with their lives in the fulfillment of responsibilities. These came from the Old and New Testaments, our national history, our literature — Our Lord himself, the Blessed Virgin Mary, the young shepherd David, the saints and missionaries, Joan of Arc, George Washington, Betsy Ross, Davey Crockett, Abraham Lincoln, and so many others. It is the nature of youngsters, and indeed of all of us, to imitate people whom we admire.

If you think your children are being taught extensively about these heroes and their accomplishments, you are probably mistaken. Ask your children about these figures and see for yourself. Ask them whom they admire.

Whom do young people typically esteem, then? Increasingly, and almost exclusively, it is figures from the entertainment media and professional sports industry — sexy singers,

vulgar comedians, superficial television characters, immoral actors, arrogant athletes. The multi-
media and sports industries have skillfully
surrounded these figures with an aura of effort-
less power, a mystique immensely attractive to
children who have nobody else to admire. These
figures radiate everything that adolescents long
to be: popular, unconstrained, happy, supremely
confident — in a word, powerful.

Power isn't the same thing as virtue, of
course; but to very many youngsters who don't
know the difference, it's close enough.

The effects of this bogus example-giving —
saturated as it is with eroticism, rebellion, and
unrestrained self-indulgence — can hardly be
exaggerated. Our experience has been that children who have little deep respect for their parents are the ones who fall headlong into the pop
culture, with all that this implies. Youngsters
who see their parents as mere "consumers,"
permissive and comfort-loving dullards, latch
on readily to the culture's joyous, libidinal
mayhem.

Adolescents who've never learned to distin-
guish mores from morals (that is, fashions that
are adoptable, as opposed to those that are always wrong) can pattern themselves after the
entire rock persona: hair, dress, sex, drugs, mili-

tant sloth, shapeless and mumbling verbiage, the whole thing.

No teenagers today are wholly unaffected by this culture. The music and personalities are everywhere. But youngsters with a firm character-upbringing (that is, youngsters who respect the evident strengths of their parents and other adults) are much less swayed by the pop-culture allurements. They may, to some extent, adopt the hair and costumes. And they may listen to a lot of music and profess preference for some groups. But by and large they know it's really theatrical sham, and they shy away from what they know is wrong.

What we want to emphasize here is the key difference between these two adolescent groups: the respect for parents as moral leaders. Children who've always respected their parents' moral strength remain virtually untouched by the drug-sex culture. Children who've never experienced this leadership, by word and example, are simply live bait.

What about single-parent homes? What hope is there for the valiant parent, usually the mother, who tries so hard to raise her children right? Our experience in this is very encouraging — surprisingly so.

In a single-parent home, the children are

much more likely to see suffering, self-sacrifice, moral courage, reliance on God's help, and serious efforts to form character and conscience. Life is very hard for divorced and widowed mothers. But their example of steadfast, heroic love can have a profound effect on the children's moral makeup. There is plenty of reason for hope. Here, as elsewhere in our discussion, everything seems to depend on parental character.

In Summary:
What to do?

We said at the outset that there are no easy answers to the questions raised here. Our purpose was to provoke serious reflection and discussion between parents, the framework for a strategy of action.

Perhaps you've decided that some aspects of your family life need reform. The children need more deliberate formation in character. Where do we go from here? What can we do?

The people who can help you best in this matter — who can give you concrete advice shaped to your personal circumstances — are other, more experienced parents. These you will have to seek out for yourselves.

The best we can do from here is to offer some general guidelines and principles, most of them implied in what you've read already. You can return to these matters again and again, discussing and refining their applications to your family, and fleshing out plans with sound advice from your friends.

In general terms, then, here's what we recommend:

1. Pray a lot for your children.
When all is said and done, your children

belong to God. He made them. He loves them more than you do. He gave them to you on loan. Someday he will call them home again. In the meantime, he entrusts them to your care. All he asks of you is that you try your best to raise them in his loving friendship.

You can't do this alone. You need his ongoing help; and, as he said repeatedly, this is yours for the asking. So ask confidently in prayer.

One of the finest things you can teach your children is a habit of personal prayer. Children raised to have a loving confidence in God very seldom go seriously wrong, not for long, not permanently. In any event, after age 14 they are pretty much out of your effective control. They are entirely in God's hands. Will they know this?

2. Formulate with each other a clear and well-thought-out picture of what kind of adults you want your children, with God's help, to become. When they're in their 20's, what sort of character will they display in religious commitment, knowledge of right and wrong, self-control, considerateness for others, sound judgment, personal toughness? What should their spouses and friends find in them to admire?

With this vision in mind, you work backwards to the details of family life today. Then you can act. If you keep this picture before you, refining it with time and basing it on prayer, you are more than half-way to your goal already.

3. Inevitably when you do this, you find much to reform in your own personal life. You are conscious of how you appear to your children — how you yourselves live religious commitment, self-control, knowledge of right and wrong, and the rest of it. Don't be dismayed by what you find lacking.

The children, after all, are not looking for success or perfection in you. They have no way of evaluating these things. What they do notice, and increasingly respect and appreciate, is that you try. To earnestly try to become better takes strength and sometimes courage. It is your ongoing struggle that will impress your children, not the results. In a real sense, they will be the results. They may, God willing, outdo you in strength of character, maybe even in sanctity.

4. Be confident of your authority. Parenthood is not an elective office. You don't have to curry popularity with your children. Your rights of leadership come with the job. Though at times you may have questions about the rightness of your decisions, your right to make the decisions should be unquestioned. The children will sometimes chafe under this stance of yours, but they will come to respect it, and you. Besides, abrasion is useful for smoothing rough surfaces, giving them a polished perfection.

When you must correct your children, reflect that you're building their strength and lifelong happiness. In this way, you will not be correcting merely for peace and quiet here and now, in other words, for your own convenience. Correcting for the sake of your own convenience leads to unclear standards, inconsistent punishments and rewards, and an overinfluence of sentiment in the children's moral judgment.

An ad-hoc control of behavior may work, more or less, when the children are very small. It will have zero influence when they're adolescents. Thinking long-term means harder work when the children are young, but it pays off when they're older.

In other words, aim to win the children's respect, not merely their affection. Tears dry up, and hurt feelings eventually go away; what must remain is respect for your steadfast and loving authority. Without this respect, they could have trouble with all other authority — God's law, teachers and employers, the civil law, and even their own conscience. This is no exaggeration.

If you are weary of exercising authority this way, remember this for the children's sake: The worst tyranny your children could possibly experience would be an inability to control themselves. Nothing causes more anguish to adolescents than having some part of their life completely out of control.

5. Make clear to your older children that you trust their integrity but not always their judgment. This is an important distinction. Unless you are given reason to do otherwise, you will always put faith in their honesty and good intentions. But you also realize that they can do serious damage to themselves through lack of experience, through immature judgment. (Just as they would not entrust their fragile valuables to younger brothers and sisters.)

Explain calmly that you have every confidence they will grow, over time, in powers of experienced and mature decision-making. You look forward to that time in their lives; you can't wait for them to grow up, literally. Until such time, you must exercise control. When they demonstrate mature responsibility, you will give them proportionate freedom — not before.

The key thing here is your manifest expectations of the children. You show them clearly that you do not want or expect them to remain as "protected" little children. On the contrary, you want them to be strong and confident men and women before they are out of their teens. You are proud of the strengths of character you see growing within them. You're confident that, with God's help, they will soon be responsible adults who live by Christian principles and can thus serve others.

6. Make your children wait for things. If possible, make them earn what they want to have. In other words, help them to "travel light" through life, confident that they can live by their wits, their ingenuity, and their patient application of concerted effort. He who needs few material things is always rich. Help them to see that comfort and convenience are only by-products of a successful life, not its purpose.

One of the most useful things you can give your children is a calendar. Teach them to plan for events, to mark the passage of time, to see cause-and-effect relationships. Teach them, in other words, that if we don't work to control events, then they control us. When your children have learned how neglect, like bad mistakes, can have grave consequences, they will learn a great deal about responsibility.

And teach them compassion and considerateness. Never tolerate gossip in your home. When they're tempted to judge others badly, help them to try to understand other people's problems and points of view. So much quarreling in the world is caused through misunderstanding. Charity doesn't mean donating old clothes; it means mostly compassionate understanding.

Finally, teach them to have gratitude. It is the basis for piety. "Please" and "thank you" must become habitual. The children simply must respect the rights and dignity of everyone, especially people in authority. Ask them frequently to pray for the family and for all those in need. Nothing is more beautiful to God than the prayers of children, and prayer is a significant contribution they can make at this age. Let them see how highly you value it.

7. Actively seek out the experienced advice of other parents. They can help you enormously. In your parish or neighborhood, you can find people who've obviously done well with their children. Befriend these families and ask them frankly how they did it.

You may find, as many parents have, that organized discussion groups are enjoyable and enlightening. At the very least, they are a source of hope. Over time, you can contribute a lot yourselves. Many people, maybe more than you think, will look upon your family life with envy and admiration.

8. Last of all, be confident of your ultimate success.

Your serious commitment to your children's growth in character is already a substantial victory. The campaign for your children's earthly and eternal happiness is a long and arduous one, but you've already won the opening decisive battle. Tactical mistakes are less important than a clear and determined strategy. As long as you keep your ideals clear before you, you can afford to make small mistakes.

Be realistic about the forces that threaten your children, but don't adopt a defensive "sandbag mentality." Your task is not to shield the children from evil, but rather to form in them the strengths to combat it effectively all their lives. Put your trust in God, your own common sense, and the advise of sensible people who share your principles. Millions of parents before you had nothing but these things, and they succeeded in raising their children well. So can you.

Your children must see you confident in this challenge, positively enjoying the adventure of raising a family. Confident people are enjoyable to live with. We naturally tend to imitate them. If your children see you steadfast in your faith and strong in your convictions, they will have a model for their own lives as adults. Your own character will be the measure by which they judge their peers.

Index

Personal Notes